Cool
Theme Parties

Perfect Party Planning for Kids

Karen Latchana Kenney

A Division of ABDO

ABDO
Publishing Company

visit us at www.abdopublishing.com

Published by ABDO Publishing Company, a division of ABDO, P.O. Box 398166, Minneapolis, Minnesota 55439. Copyright © 2012 by Abdo Consulting Group, Inc. International copyrights reserved in all countries. No part of this book may be reproduced in any form without written permission from the publisher. Checkerboard Library™ is a trademark and logo of ABDO Publishing Company.

Printed in the United States of America, North Mankato, Minnesota
052011
092011

♻ PRINTED ON RECYCLED PAPER

Interior Design and Production: Colleen Dolphin, Mighty Media, Inc.
Cover Design: Aaron DeYoe
Series Editor: Liz Salzmann
Photo Credits: Colleen Dolphin, Shutterstock

The following manufacturers/names appearing in this book are trademarks:
Betty Crocker® Potato Buds®, Glue Dots® Adhesive Dots, Morton® Salt,
Old London® Seasoned Bread Crumbs, Paper Mate® Sharpwriter

Library of Congress Cataloging-in-Publication Data

Kenney, Karen Latchana.
  Cool theme parties : perfect party planning for kids / Karen Latchana Kenney.
      p. cm. -- (Cool parties)
  Includes index.
  ISBN 978-1-61714-978-8
  1. Children's parties--Planning--Juvenile literature. I. Title.
  GV1205.K48 2012
  793.2'1--dc22
                                    2011004215

Contents

It's Theme Party Time!

It's time to host a party! Why not have a theme? Make it a Hawaiian Luau or a Rockin' Rock Star party. Pick whatever you think is cool. All the elements of your party can go with that theme. It will be a blast!

But to make this party happen, you need to plan out the **details**. Start with the basics, like the *when* and *where* of the party. Then move on to details like decorations and **menus**. Create some cool invitations and send them out. And don't forget to plan the activities! They keep the party moving at a fun pace.

Remember to plan and do as much as you can before the party starts. It takes time and hard work to be a host. But it's definitely worth it! Then all that's left for you to do is have fun!

Safety

◎ Ask for an adult's help when making food for your party.

◎ Find out where you can make crafts and play games. Do you need to protect a table surface? What should you use?

◎ Check the party room. Can anything be broken easily? Ask a parent to remove it before the party.

Permission

◎ Where in the house can you have the party? Are any rooms off-limits?

◎ How much money can you spend? Where can you shop and who will take you?

◎ Make sure guests' parents know who will be overseeing the party.

◎ Can you put up decorations? How?

◎ How long should the party last? When should guests go home?

◎ Talk about who will clean up after the party.

Party Planning Basics

Every great party has the same basic **details**. They are the *who, what, when,* and *where* of the party. Your party planning should begin with these basics. Then make lists of everything you need to buy, make, and do for the party. You should also have a list of everyone you invited. Mark whether each guest can come or not.

Who: How many friends do you want to invite? And who will they be? Try to pick friends who will get along and have fun.

What: What is the theme party for? Is it your birthday? Or just for fun? You'll need to explain this on the invitation.

When: Parties are best on the weekends. Pick a Saturday or Sunday. But don't plan the party on a weekend with a holiday.

Where: Is the party at your house, at a park, or at a party room? Explain the details to your guests. And don't forget to include directions!

Favors:

What to buy:

What to make:

Activities:

What to buy:

What to make:

Menu:

Decorations:

What to buy:

What to make:

Music:

Equipment:

Guests:

_____ yes/no

_____ yes/no

_____ yes/no

_____ yes/no

_____ yes/no

_____ yes/no

7

What's Your Theme?

You've decided to host a theme party. You just have to pick your theme! Do you like to read books about wizards? Maybe you should have a magic party. Do you like to be fun and silly? You could have a backwards party. Whatever you pick, it should be a theme that fits what you like!

Once you've picked a theme, plan all the **details** around that theme. For example, you can make wands as favors for a wizard party. Or make upside-down decorations for a backwards party. It's fun to try to make the party details match the theme! Check out the party themes on the next page. There are activities in this book to match each one.

Detective

If you like searching for clues, this party is for you! Plan mysteries for guests to solve. See what they figure out from the clues!

Vampire

Make your own vampire world for this party. Drink blood-red cranberry juice. Then share your favorite vampire stories.

Magic

This party is about wizards, **potions**, and spells. Pretend to be wizards and make up spells. Then try making some cool potions!

Hawaiian

A Hawaiian party is **tropical** and fun. Wear grass skirts and sway to **ukulele** music. You can even do the **limbo**!

Backwards

Things are not what they seem at this party. Say things backwards. Wear your socks on your hands and your shirt inside-out. See how weird it can get!

Rock Star

Get glammed up for this party. Dress like a rock star and sing some **karaoke**. See what it's like to be in the spotlight!

Medieval

Go back in time to the days of knights and **chivalry**. Make shields and use swords. Call everyone "m'lady" and "sir." Just pretend to be **medieval**!

Don't forget...

After you pick your theme, let guests know all about it. Do they need to bring something or wear special clothes? Let them know on the invitation. That way guests will show up prepared. They'll also be even more excited to party!

Tools & Supplies

Here are some of the things you'll need to do the activities in this book:

cupcake liners

muffin tin

salt

pepper

bowl

shredded cheese

food coloring

craft sticks

tablecloth

measuring cups

mixing bowls

instant mashed potatoes

metal tongs

mixing spoon

dish soap

measuring spoons

egg

ground beef

Italian bread crumbs

10

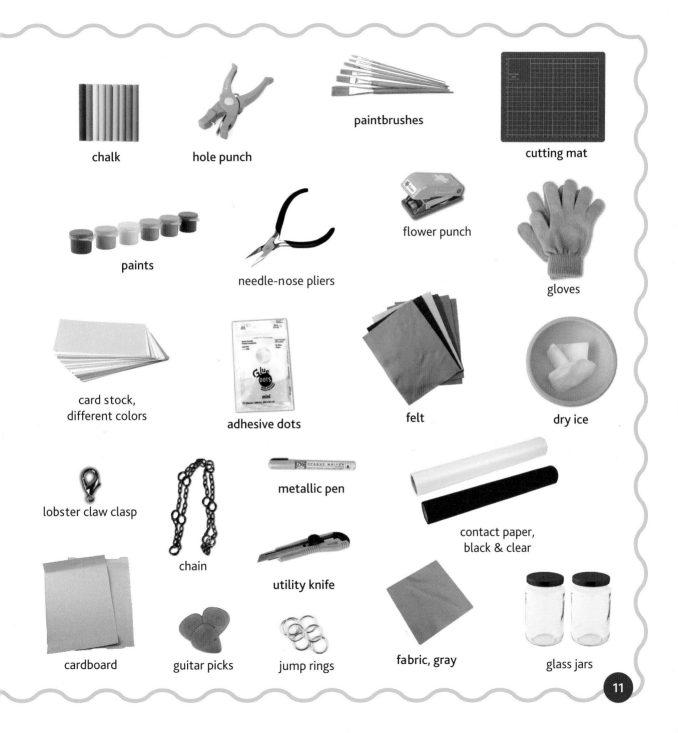

chalk

hole punch

paintbrushes

cutting mat

paints

needle-nose pliers

flower punch

gloves

card stock,
different colors

adhesive dots

felt

dry ice

lobster claw clasp

chain

metallic pen

contact paper,
black & clear

utility knife

cardboard

guitar picks

jump rings

fabric, gray

glass jars

11

Lovely Lei Invitation

The perfect invite for a Hawaiian party!

What You Need

card stock, different colors
scissors
ruler
flower punch
hole punch
adhesive dots
metallic pen

Hawaiian Theme

1 Cut out a 5 x 7-inch (13 x 18 cm) piece of card stock. Then fold it in half.

2 Make the flowers using the paper flower punch. Use the circular paper hole punch for the center of the flowers. Use bright and fun colors. And make equal numbers of flowers and flower centers.

3 Arrange the flowers in a wreath on the front of the card. Then put the flower centers on top of each flower. This is the lei.

4 Stick the flowers in place with the adhesive dots. Try to get the centers in the middle of the flowers.

5 Write the party announcement in the middle of the lei. Make it fun and simple, like "Let's Luau!" Open up the card and write the party **details** inside. Add a few flowers around the borders.

More Ideas!

DETECTIVE THEME
Make a "top-secret" invitation for your guests. Cut up file folders to make the cards. Then stick them in manila envelopes. Print "TOP SECRET" on the envelopes.

ROCK STAR THEME
Cut your invitations into star shapes. Write the details in the middle using glitter pens. Put glue around the edges of the star. Shake glitter on the edges.

MEDIEVAL THEME
Make a card with a pop-up piece inside. Cut out a castle or shield shape from card stock. Color it and then glue it to the pop-up piece.

Spooky Wall Decals

Stick these spooky decals on your walls!

14

Vampire Theme

 1 Draw a large and a small bat shape on card stock. Start with circles for the bodies. Draw a wing on each side of the circles. Then add two pointed ears at the top of each circle.

 2 Draw a tombstone shape on card stock. Draw a rectangle, but make one short end rounded.

 3 Cut out all three shapes. These are your **templates**. Unroll the contact paper and tape the templates to it.

 4 Cut around the templates. Make as many bats and tombstones as you want. Peel the backing off and stick the **decals** to the wall.

 5 Use chalk to write "R.I.P." on the tombstones. Draw eyes on the bats.

More Ideas!

DETECTIVE THEME
Make a mystery crime scene at your party. Draw footprints on black paper. Cut them out and tape them to the floor. Draw a chalk body outline on the sidewalk.

BACKWARDS THEME
Blow up balloons. Tie long pieces of ribbon to the balloons. Then tape the ends of the ribbons to the ceiling. Lay streamers on the floor.

ROCK STAR THEME
Cut guitar and star shapes out of card stock. Paint them with glitter glue. String them onto a long ribbon to make a banner. Hang it on the wall.

Rockin' Guitar Pick Chain

Give these out as super cool party favors!

16

Rock Star Theme

1 Punch holes in four guitar picks. Hold one tightly and punch a hole near the flat edge of the pick. Repeat with the other picks.

2 Use jump rings to connect the guitar picks to the chain link. Pull a jump ring open slightly. Put it through the hole in one of the picks.

3 Put the jump ring through a hole in the chain. Squeeze the ring shut with the pliers.

4 Attach the other picks in the same way. Make sure the space between the picks on the chain is even. Each pick should hang from the chain.

5 Use a jump ring to attach the lobster clasp to one end of the chain. Add a jump ring to the other end of the chain. Close it tightly. Connect the clasp to the ring to wear the necklace. What a rockin' necklace!

More Ideas!

HAWAIIAN THEME
Make paper leis. Cut flower shapes out of paper. Use bright colors. Punch a hole in the middle of each shape. Then string the flowers onto a ribbon. Tie a knot between each flower.

MAGIC THEME
Give your guests magic wands! Color wooden dowels with markers. Make **unique designs** on each wand. Then wrap a ribbon around one end of each wand.

MEDIEVAL THEME
Turn plastic wine glasses into goblets. Paint them with gold or silver paint. Glue jewels onto the sides. Then paint each guest's name on a goblet.

What's on the Menu?

A great party isn't complete without delicious snacks and cool drinks! It's best to make finger foods. They are fun to eat and easy to carry. Everyone can still mingle while they snack. To plan your party **menu**, think about a few things first.

Variety

Everyone has different tastes. Make sure you have some sweet and some salty things. Have healthy choices and **vegetarian** dishes too.

Meals

Will your party last a long time? You will need more than just snacks if it does. Think about the time of day when your party will take place. Will your guests need breakfast, lunch, or dinner? And maybe they'll want snacks too!

Amount

How many people are coming? Plan to have enough food to feed everyone.

Time

It takes time to shop for and prepare food. Pick recipes that you have time to make. Remember, there are other things you need to do before the party.

Allergies

Check with your guests to see if they have any food **allergies**. Make sure there are things those guests can eat.

Sample Party Menus

It's fun to plan your menu around your party theme. Here are some examples.

Very Curious Detective Menu

Mystery Fruit Ball Salad

Veggie Spy-ral Rolls

Puzzle Piece–Shaped Sandwiches

Question Mark Cookies

Strangely Orange Milk

Dessert First Backwards Menu

Upside Down Juice Boxes

Kooky Cupcakes*
*recipe on page 22!

Spaghetti Served on Sauce

Cheese-Filled Baguette

Lettuce Wrap Sandwich

Knightly Medieval Menu

Strawberries and Grapes

Cheese and Honey on Soda Bread

Sticky Honey-glazed Chicken Legs

Mini Apple Tarts

Spiced Apple Cider

Watch Out for Vampire Bites Menu

Wooden Staked Tomatoes & Mozzarella

Garlicky Breadsticks and Dipping Sauce

Ripe Watermelon Cubes

Rich Red Velvet Cake

Cranberry Juice Punch

Ask for help finding easy and delicious recipes to make.

Kooky Cupcakes

Meatloaf cupcakes are totally backwards!

What You Need

muffin tin
cupcake liners
measuring cups and spoons
mixing bowls and spoons
fork
1 pound lean ground beef
½ cup Italian bread crumbs
1 cup shredded cheese
3 tbsp ketchup
1 egg
½ tsp salt
½ tsp pepper
instant mashed potatoes
food coloring
sprinkles (optional)

BackwardsTheme

 1 Set the oven to 375 degrees. Then line the muffin tin cups with the cupcake liners.

 2 Mix together the meat, bread crumbs, shredded cheese, ketchup, egg, salt, and pepper. Make sure everything is combined well.

 3 Spoon the meatloaf mixture into the cupcake liners. Divide it evenly. Then smooth the tops of each one. Remember, you want them to look like cupcakes!

 4 Put the muffin tin on the middle rack of the oven. Be sure to get help with this. The oven is very hot! Bake the cupcakes for 15 minutes.

 5 Make three cups of mashed potatoes. Follow the directions on the box. Then mix a few drops of food coloring into the mashed potatoes. You could also make different colored cupcakes. Just divide the mashed potatoes into 2 or 3 bowls and use a different food coloring in each one.

 6 Put a spoonful of mashed potatoes on each cupcake. Smooth it so it looks like frosting. If you want, put some sprinkles on top.

7 Be sure to serve the cupcakes when they are still warm. Your friends will be so surprised!

Show Me Your Badge

Every good detective needs a badge!

What You Need

pictures of your guests
card stock
ruler
scissors
pens
glue sticks
clear contact paper

Detective Badge

Inspector C. Luze
Dept. of Mysterious Flying Fruit

Detective Badge

Detective Ida Solver
Secret Office of Unsolved Bug Crimes

Detective Theme

 1   On your invitation, ask guests to bring 2 x 2-inch (5 x 5 cm) pictures of themselves.

 2   Before the party, cut 4 x 3-inch (10 x 8 cm) rectangles out of card stock. Make one for each guest. And don't forget about your own badge!

 3   Draw a 2 x 2-inch (5 x 5 cm) square on each card. Put it in the upper left corner. Write "Detective Badge" beside the square. Then draw writing lines below using a ruler.

4   At the party, have each guest glue his or her picture over the square on a card. Then ask each guest to write his or her detective name and special detective department. Make the names funny and **unique**!

 5   Take the backing off two pieces of clear contact paper. Place the cards on the sticky side of one sheet. Stick the second sheet on top. Start at one side and smooth it over the cards. Then cut around the cards.

More Ideas!

VAMPIRE THEME
Make a vampire cape using a piece of black fabric. Glue Velcro halves to two corners to hold it on around your neck. Paint spooky bats on the cape. Use glow-in-the dark paint.

HAWAIIAN THEME
Have a fun **limbo** contest! Use a broom as the limbo stick. Play fun beach party music. Then see how low you can go!

MAGIC THEME
Teach guests a fun magic trick. Try the ball and three cups trick. Show them once. Then let everyone try to trick each other!

Magic Bubble Potion

Try this mysterious trick at your magic party!

What You Need

- dry ice
- gloves
- bowl
- tablecloth
- glass jars, one per guest
- craft sticks, one per guest
- pitcher of water
- dish soap
- food coloring
- metal tongs

MagicTheme

 1 Ask an adult to help with the dry ice. And don't forget to wear gloves when touching it! Break the dry ice into small pieces that can fit inside the glass jars. Then put the dry ice in a bowl. Store it in the freezer.

 2 Cover the table you are using with a tablecloth. Then set out a glass jar and craft stick for each guest.

 3 Ask each guest to sit by a jar. Fill the jars halfway with water. Then pass around the dish soap. Tell your guests to squirt soap into their jars.

4 Have guests put a few drops of food coloring into their jars. They can use one color or try a combination. Then they should stir their **potions** with the craft sticks.

 5 Remove the dry ice from the freezer. Use the tongs to drop a piece into each guest's jar. Ask them to stir their potions. Then watch the bubbles spill from the jars!

More Ideas!

BACKWARDS THEME
Play a backwards guessing game. Spell words backwards on pieces of paper. Have one person say the backwards word. Then see if anyone can guess what the real word is!

HAWAIIAN THEME
Make your own hula skirts! Just tie long pieces of raffia to a rope. Fill up the rope to make a full skirt. Tie the rope around your waist.

ROCK STAR THEME
Try singing rock **karaoke**. Find a few karaoke CDs. Look up the words to songs on the Internet and print them. Give them to your guests. Then sing!

Medieval Shield

Guests will love making these unique shields!

What You Need

- 12 x 12-inch (30 x 30 cm) pieces of cardboard, 1 per guest
- ruler
- pencils
- scissors
- paints
- paintbrushes
- pictures of dragons and lions
- glue
- felt
- utility knife
- cutting mat
- 2 x 12-inch (5 x 30 cm) strips of gray fabric, 2 per guest

MedievalTheme

 1 Draw the shape of a shield on the cardboard. Cut it out. Draw your **design** on the shield. Most shields have four sections with a **symbol** in the middle. You can draw the symbol or plan to glue one on later. Paint the shield. Let the paint dry for an hour. Glue on any symbols or other decorations.

 2 Cut a piece of felt 3 inches (8 cm) wide and as long as the top of the shield. Make cuts along the felt. Stop about ½ inch (1 cm) from the edge. Glue the top of the felt **fringe** to the shield.

 3 Cut two 2-inch (5 cm) slits near one side of the shield. The slits should be about 1 inch (3 cm) apart. Cut two more slits on the other side.

 4 Use two strips of fabric to make handles. Push the end of one strip through a slit from the back to the front. Push it down through the other slit. Tie the ends of the fabric together. Do the same thing with the other strip of fabric and the other pair of slits. To use the shield, put your arm through the fabric loops.

More Ideas!

BACKWARDS THEME
Hold a backwards fashion show! Gather clothes and accessories for your friends to try on. Then give each person one minute to make a weird backwards outfit!

MAGIC THEME
Dress like a wizard with a hat! Make it from black card stock. Then add star stickers. Or paint it with cool colors.

VAMPIRE THEME
Show your vampire style with a bat charm. Make it from polymer clay. Add a metal hook at the top. Bake it. Then attach it to your backpack or key chain!

Conclusion

What a great theme party! Fun crafts! Good food! But the party room is a mess! There's still work to do. Make sure you clean up and put everything back in order. Your parents will see what a responsible party host you are.

Was it your birthday? Did you keep track of your gifts? It's important to write down who gave you what. That will make sending thank-you cards easier. Make thank-you cards that match the party's theme. Write something **unique** and personal on each guest's card. It will make your friends feel special. Then send out the cards within a week after the party.

Hosting a party is hard work! There are so many **details** to plan and things to make. In the end, though, it all comes together to make a party to remember! Theme parties are fun, so what will your next party be? Check out the other books in the *Cool Parties* series for great ideas.

Glossary

allergy – sickness caused by touching, breathing, or eating certain things.

chivalry – the code of honor and conduct followed by knights.

decal – a label or sticker with a picture or design on it.

design – a decorative pattern or arrangement.

detail – a small part of something.

fringe – a border made up of hanging strips or threads.

karaoke – an activity in which people sing songs while a machine plays the music.

limbo – a dance where you bend backwards to go under a bar or pole.

medieval – related to the Middle Ages, the period from AD 500 to 1500.

menu – a list of things to choose from.

potion – liquids mixed together to make a medicine or poison.

symbol – an object or picture that stands for or represents something.

template – a shape you draw or cut around to copy it onto something else.

tropical – like or related to the hottest areas on earth.

ukulele – a type of small guitar that is popular in Hawaii.

unique – different, unusual, or special.

vegetarian – without any meat.

Web Sites

To learn more about cool parties, visit ABDO Publishing Company on the World Wide Web at **www.abdopublishing.com**. Web sites about cool parties are featured on our book links page. These links are routinely monitored and updated to provide the most current information available.

Index